Super Science Projects
About Earth's
Soil and Water

ROBERT GARDNER

ILLUSTRATIONS BY TOM LABAFF

Enslow Elementary
an imprint of

 Enslow Publishers, Inc.
40 Industrial Road
Box 398
Berkeley Heights, NJ 07922
USA

http://www.enslow.com

Enslow Elementary, an imprint of Enslow Publishers, Inc.

Enslow Elementary® is a registered trademark of Enslow Publishers, Inc.

Library of Congress Cataloging-in-Publication Data

Gardner, Robert, 1929–
    Super science projects about Earth's soil and water / Robert Gardner.
      p. cm. — (Rockin' earth science experiments)
    Includes bibliographical references and index.
    ISBN-13: 978-0-7660-2735-0
    ISBN-10: 0-7660-2735-X
    1. Soils—Experiments—Juvenile literature. 2. Water—Experiments—Juvenile literature. 3. Science projects—Juvenile literature. I. Title. II. Series: Gardner, Robert, 1929– . Rockin' earth science experiments.
    S591.3.G37 2005
    631.4078—dc22

                                                    2006006680

Printed in the United States of America

10 9 8 7 6 5 4 3 2

Illustration credits: Tom LaBaff

Photo credits: © Folio/Omni-Photo Communications, Inc., p. 21; Atlas Copco, p. 32; Bertil Lindén (www.chitambo.com), p. 12; Novosti Press Agency/Photo Researchers, Inc., p. 8; Herman Eisenbeiss/Photo Researchers, Inc., p. 41; Ken Hammond/Agricultural Research Service, USDA, p. 36; Lyn Topinka/US Geological Survey, p. 24; Photo by Lynn Betts, USDA, Natural Resources Conservation Service, p. 44; US Geological Survey, p. 16; Wil Ellis, p. 28.

Cover photo: © 2006 Jupiter Images Corporation

Contents

Experiments with a 🎖 symbol feature **Ideas for Your Science Fair.**

Introduction

You may be surprised to learn that you can walk on water. It is true because there is water in the ground you walk on. In this book you will learn about soil and water by doing experiments. You will discover that water is always on the move. It can move from the ground into the air. But then it falls back to Earth as rain. You will learn about the different types of soil. You will see how water can move soil. You will watch seeds grow in different soils. You will learn about all these things and much, much more.

Entering a Science Fair

Most of the experiments in this book (those marked with a 🎖 symbol) have ideas for science fair projects. However, judges at science fairs like experiments that are creative, so do not simply copy an experiment from this book. Start with one of the ideas suggested and make a project of your own. Choose something you really like and want to know more about. It will be more interesting to you. And it can lead to a creative experiment that you plan and carry out.

Before entering a science fair, read one or more of the books about this subject listed under Further Reading. They will give you helpful hints and lots of useful information about science fairs.

Safety First

To do experiments safely, always follow these rules.

1 Always do experiments under adult supervision.

2 Read all instructions carefully. If you have questions, check with the adult.

3 Be serious when experimenting. Fooling around can be dangerous to you and to others.

4 Keep the area where you work clean and organized. When you have finished, clean up and put your materials away.

Does Water Ever Disappear?

What do think will happen to a drop of water left open to the air? Write down your ideas and your reasons for them.

THINGS YOU WILL NEED:

- teaspoon
- water
- medicine cup
- blue food coloring
- aluminum foil
- eyedropper
- petroleum jelly

Now Let's Find Out!

1 Put one teaspoonful of water in a medicine cup. Add two drops of blue food coloring to the water.

2 Place a smooth piece of aluminum foil on a counter. Using an eyedropper, put two separate drops of the blue water on the aluminum foil. The drops should be at least 2 inches (5 centimeters) apart.

3 Empty the medicine cup. Cover the rim of the cup with petroleum jelly. Then turn the cup upside down. Put it over one of the drops. The jelly should make an air-tight seal around the drop.

6

4 Rinse the eyedropper with water. Then place a drop of clear water on the aluminum foil.

5 Look at all three drops every hour or so throughout the day. What changes take place? Can you explain the changes you see?

aluminum foil

Does Water Ever Disappear?
An Explanation

The uncovered drops slowly disappeared. Why? Because liquid water slowly changes to a gas and mixes with air. We say it evaporates. Only a small amount of the covered drop evaporated. There was not enough air around it to take up even a drop of water.

Particles of liquid water are close together. But they are moving. The faster-moving ones break away from the others. They move apart, become a gas, and mix with air.

FACT: Salt can be obtained from salty sea water. The water evaporates. The salt is left behind just as the blue food coloring was. Often, the sun's heat is used to evaporate the water faster.

These large machines remove salt from seawater.

The solid blue dye (food coloring) was left on the aluminum. The dye particles do not move fast enough to separate from one another. After the water evaporated, the dye was left behind.

Ideas for Your Science Fair

- How does temperature affect the evaporation of water?

- How does wind (moving air) affect the evaporation of water?

- How does sweating keep you cool?

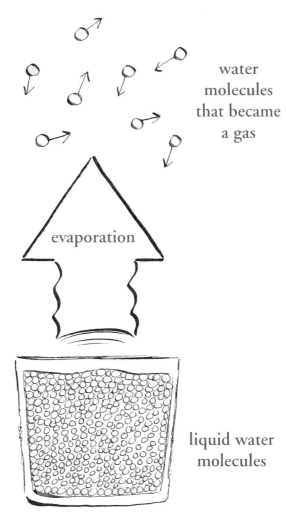

water molecules that became a gas

evaporation

liquid water molecules

2

The Water Cycle

What do you think happens to water that evaporates into the air? Write down your ideas and your reasons for them.

Now Let's Find Out!

1 Find a plastic box about the size of a shoe box. Put the box in a warm place. Let bright sunlight shine on it.

2 Add stones to one end of the box. The stones represent mountains and soil. Then add an inch or two of water. Water should cover the bottom of the box. The water represents lakes, rivers, and oceans.

3 Cover the top of the box with plastic wrap. Seal it with a rubber band as shown.

4 Look at the box now and then for several hours. Over time you will see water drops forming on the underside of the plastic wrap.

THINGS YOU WILL NEED:

- plastic box about the size of a shoe box
- plastic wrap
- stones
- water
- warm place
- bright sunlight
- rubber band

Where do you think the water came from? Write down your ideas and your reasons for them.

5 Look closely. You will see some of the drops grow bigger. They will fall as "rain" on the land and water below.

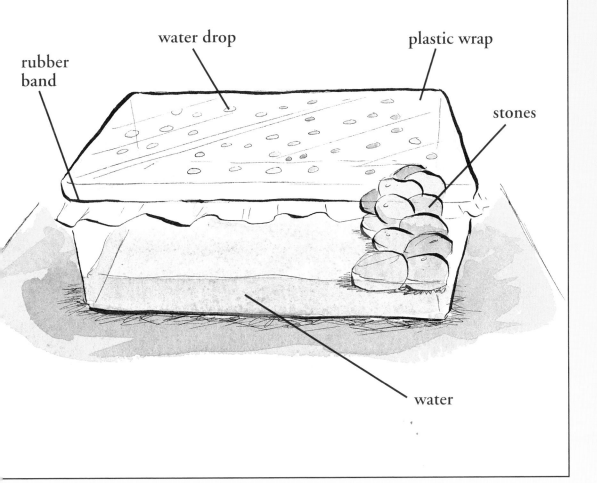

water drop

plastic wrap

rubber band

stones

water

The Water Cycle
An Explanation

You made a model of the water cycle. Water evaporates from Earth's surface. It enters the air as a gas. When the gas cools, the particles of water move slower. These slower particles bump into one another. They may stick together and become tiny droplets of water. The tiny droplets form clouds. These droplets may grow and fall as raindrops. All of Earth's water eventually falls as rain. And all this water will eventually evaporate again. It is called a cycle because it happens over and over again.

FACT: Every year 122,000 cubic miles (134,000 trillion gallons) of water evaporate. All that water enters Earth's atmosphere. The same amount of water falls back to Earth as rain.

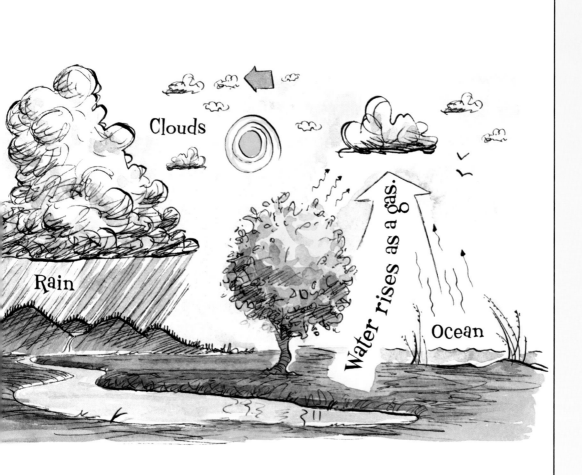

Clouds

Rain

Water rises as a gas.

Ocean

Idea for Your Science Fair

- Design your own way of showing how the water cycle works.

3

Looking at Soil

What do you think makes up soil? Write down your ideas and your reasons for them.

Now Let's Find Out!

1 Ask an adult to help you dig a hole in a field, garden, or safe open space. Make your hole one foot or more deep, so that you can see its sides. Look at the sides of the hole. Can you see layers of soil? Do the layers have different colors? What is the color of the top layer?

2 Collect a sample of soil from each layer. Put the samples in clear plastic cups. Label the cups with the layer and take them home with you.

3 Feel the soil samples. Do any feel gritty? Sticky? Smooth?

THINGS YOU WILL NEED:

- **an adult**
- shovel
- field, garden, or safe open space
- clear plastic cups
- marking pen
- white paper
- magnifying glass
- water

4 Spread a small amount of soil from each sample on a sheet of white paper. Use a magnifying glass to look at the soils. What do you see? Do some samples have bigger particles than others?

5 Slowly pour water into the cups that hold the soil samples. What do you observe? Do you see bubbles coming out of the soil? What do you think might be causing the bubbles? Write down your ideas and your reasons for them.

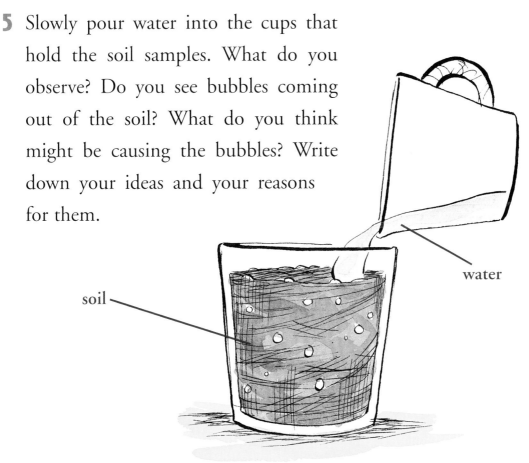

water

soil

Looking at Soil
An Explanation

Most soils are layered. The top layer (topsoil) is usually dark. It contains the remains of living things—rotted leaves, bark, dead plants. These remains are called *organic matter*. Subsoils are usually lighter.

FACT: Soil particles are formed by the weathering of rocks. Weathering is caused by water, wind, temperature changes, and other things. It slowly breaks rocks into small particles.

Soil is made from rocks that have broken into tiny particles. Sandy soil feels gritty. It has the largest soil particles. Silty soil feels smooth. Soil with lots of clay feels sticky. Its particles are very small.

When you added water to the soils, you

probably saw bubbles of air come out. Air was between the soil particles. The water pushed the air out. Good soil contains air. Plant roots need the air to live.

Ideas for Your Science Fair

- What fraction of dry sand is actually air? Do an experiment to find out.

- Measure the depth of topsoil in different places. Where is it deepest? Least deep? Can you explain why?

4

Water and Soils

Soil must hold water for plants to grow. What types of soil do you think hold water the best? Write down your ideas and your reasons for them.

THINGS YOU WILL NEED:

- different soils such as sand, gravel, potting soil, topsoil, clay, and garden soil
- newspapers
- warm, dry place
- large (8-oz) paper or Styrofoam cups
- clear plastic cups
- nail
- measuring cup
- marking pen
- wooden coffee stirrers or Popsicle sticks

Now Let's Find Out!

1 Collect different soils such as sand, gravel, potting soil, topsoil, clay, and garden soil.

2 Put several cups of each soil on separate newspapers. Spread the soils. Let them dry in a warm place for a week.

3 Find a paper cup for each soil. Use a nail to punch holes in and around the bottom centers of the cups (see drawing). Label each paper cup with the name of the soil it will hold. Measure one cup of each dry soil and place it into its paper cup.

4 Put each cup of soil on top of an empty, clear, plastic cup as shown. Wooden coffee stirrers or Popsicle sticks can support the cups. Put the supports under the outer edges of the cups' bottoms (see drawing).

5 Slowly pour one cup of water onto each soil. Let the extra water drip into the lower cups. Once the dripping stops, look at the water levels in each clear cup. Which soil soaked up the most water? The least water?

bottom of the cup that holds soil

soil inside paper or Styrofoam cup

Water and Soils
An Explanation

Clay holds water very well. Soils with lots of clay hold a lot of water. Sand and gravel do not hold water well. Gravel and sandy soil are used for good drainage. They let water run through them. Potting soil, topsoil, and garden soil hold

grass

topsoil

gravel

water and allow plants to grow. How much they hold depends on the amount of clay they contain. Clay makes up about one-fourth ($1/4$) of soils good for growing plants.

Settling Soil

Soil is often carried away by water in streams or by floods. At some point, the particles of soil settle out of the water. What do you think will happen to soil if it is shaken up in water and then left to settle? Write down your ideas and your reasons for them.

THINGS YOU WILL NEED:

- topsoil
- subsoils
- plastic container
- tall, clear, quart jar with cap or screw-on cover
- water
- paper towel
- level surface

Now Let's Find Out!

1 Mix together some topsoil and some subsoils in a plastic container. Fill a tall, clear, quart jar about one-third of the way with the soil mixture. Then nearly fill the jar with water.

2 Put the cover on the jar. Shake the jar for one minute.

3 Put the jar on a folded paper towel on a level surface. Let the soil particles settle overnight.

Are there floaters?

Is the water cloudy?

settled soil

Did any of the soil particles float? If they did, what do you think they are?

Where are the biggest particles? The smallest?

Some particles of clay are so small they may not settle out. They will give the water a cloudy appearance. Were there tiny clay particles in the soil you tested? How do you know?

Settling Soil
An Explanation

Large, heavy particles such as gravel and sand settle out of water first. They fall faster through the water. Smaller, lighter particles of silt and clay fall more slowly. They will settle on top of the sand and gravel. If the water remains cloudy after several days, the soil contained small clay particles. These particles, like dust in air, remain mixed in or suspended in the water. You may have found small bits of organic matter floating

FACT: Rivers carry a lot of soil. Much of that soil settles out when the rivers empty into lakes or seas. These settled-out soils are called sediments. Often, large dredging machines are used to remove the sediments. This is done so boats do not get stuck in the soil.

A dredging machine removes sediment from the bottom of the water.

on the water. These would be tiny pieces of leaves, grass, wood, insects, and so on.

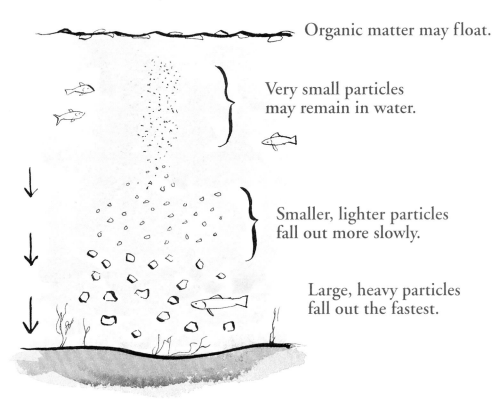

Organic matter may float.

Very small particles may remain in water.

Smaller, lighter particles fall out more slowly.

Large, heavy particles fall out the fastest.

Idea for Your Science Fair

- Find a way to measure the average size of the particles from each layer of soil that has settled.

Underground Water

How do you think water gets into a well? Write down your ideas and your reasons for them.

Now Let's Find Out!

1 Find a clear plastic dish about 4 to 5 inches (10 to 13 centimeters) deep. The bottom of the dish represents bedrock that water cannot get into or past.

2 Add about 2 inches (5 centimeters) of pea-size pebbles to the dish. Pour about an inch of sand over the pebbles. The sand and pebbles represent the soil and rocks above the bedrock.

3 Hollow out some of the soil near one side of the dish. Put water into a watering can.

THINGS YOU WILL NEED:

- clear plastic dish about 4-5 inches deep (the kind supermarkets use to package salads works well)
- pebbles
- sand
- water
- watering can (make your own by punching holes through a plastic cup)

4 Use the watering can to "rain" on the soil. Watch the water seep into the soil. What happens to the level of the water as "rain" seeps into the soil? Where does a "pond" form? Look at the water level in the pond. How does it compare with the level of the water in the soil?

"rain"

sand

underground water

"pond"

5 Let water evaporate from your pond and soil for a day or two. What happens to the water level in the soil? What happens to the pond? What happens when it "rains" again?

Underground Water
An Explanation

Rain and melted snow trickle into the ground. At some depth water fills all the spaces between soil particles and rocks. The underground soil and rocks that hold the water below this depth is called an aquifer (AK wih fur).

You made a model aquifer. The water level in the "pond" matched the water level in the underground water. When you let the water evaporate, the water level became lower. The "pond" may have dried up. This can happen during a drought. Rain will refill the aquifer.

FACT: Many farms in the western United States use windmills to pump water from an aquifer.

Aquifers provide water for many towns and farms. Wells are made by drilling into an aquifer. Homes and businesses pump water from these wells.

soil—some spaces contain water, others contain air

top of aquifer

aquifer—water fills all the spaces between soil and rocks

bedrock

Ideas for Your Science Fair 🎗

- Aquifers are sometimes stacked one on top of another. Build a model of a two-layered aquifer.

- Build a model windmill that can pump water from a pond in a model aquifer.

A Polluted Aquifer

How do you think a well gets polluted? Write down your ideas and your reasons for them.

THINGS YOU WILL NEED:

- dry sand
- clear plastic vial (30–50 mL)
- eyedropper
- water
- green food coloring

Now Let's Find Out!

1 Add dry sand to a clear plastic vial. Fill it about three-quarters full. This will become your aquifer.

2 Use an eyedropper to "rain" on the aquifer. Watch the water trickle down through the sand. Continue "raining" until a "pond" covers the aquifer.

3 Make a "well" by pushing the eyedropper to the bottom at one side of your aquifer. Use the eyedropper to "pump" water from the aquifer. Pump out as much water as possible.

4 Now "pollute" the aquifer. Add one drop of green food coloring to the sand. Then rain on the sand again. What happens to the "pollution?"

5 Pump the aquifer again. Rain on and pump the aquifer several times. Does the well become polluted?

6 Can the pollution be removed by many rains and pumpings? How might a polluted aquifer be cleaned up?

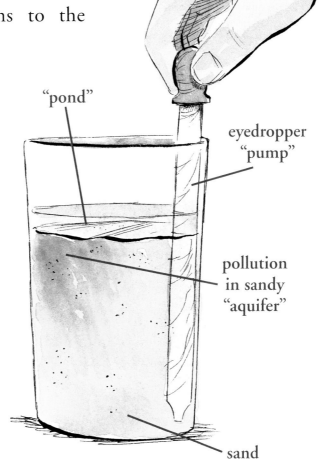

"pond"

eyedropper "pump"

pollution in sandy "aquifer"

sand

A Polluted Aquifer
An Explanation

Pesticides, fertilizers, or other poisons may be spilled on the ground. Rain falling on the polluted soil can carry the pollution into the aquifer below. Once in the aquifer, the pollution spreads. Suppose water is pumped from a well in the aquifer. Then polluted water will be drawn into the well. The polluted water may be unfit to drink.

Polluted aquifers can sometimes be cleaned. Water is added repeatedly and the polluted water is pumped out of the aquifer. Then the pollutant is removed before the water is returned to the aquifer.

FACT: Machines like this one are used to drill wells into an aquifer.

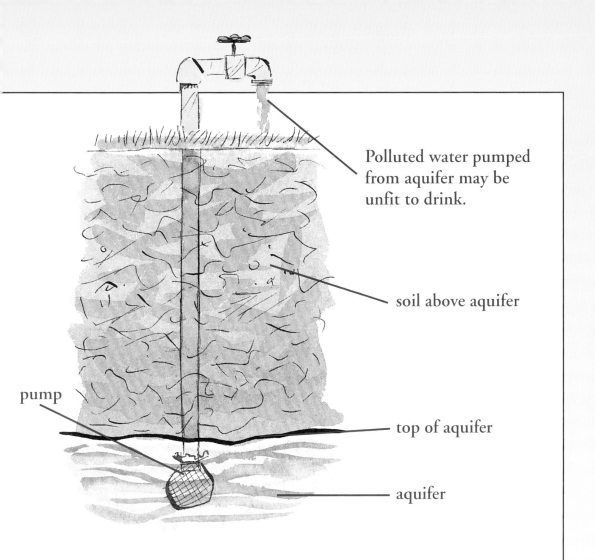

Polluted water pumped from aquifer may be unfit to drink.

soil above aquifer

pump

top of aquifer

aquifer

Ideas for Your Science Fair 🎖

- Where does the water you drink come from? How does it get to your home?

- What happens to your home's wastewater?

Soils and Plants

Do you think plants will grow better in some soils than in others? Write down your ideas and your reasons for them.

THINGS YOU WILL NEED:

- small flower pots
- soils—sand, gravel, garden soil, potting soil, and others
- large bean seeds, such as lima bean seeds
- warm sunny place
- water
- paper towels
- plastic container
- cardboard ruler
- paper
- pen or pencil

Now Let's Find Out!

1 Nearly fill several small flower pots with different soils. Use sand, gravel, garden soil, potting soil, and other soil you may have.

2 In each soil, plant two or three bean seeds about an inch deep. All soils should share the same conditions in a warm sunny place. Keep the soils damp but not wet.

3 Put several damp paper towels in a plastic container. Place a few bean seeds on the towels. Cover the seeds with more damp towels. Place a sheet of cardboard on the container.

Soil	Day	Height	
Sand	8	1.0	1.3
Gravel	8	1.2	1.6
Loam	8	1.4	1.7
Garden	8	1.1	1.8

4 Keep the towels damp. Look at the seeds every day. Do you see small plants beginning to grow from the seeds? If you do, this means the seeds have germinated.

Do seeds need soil to germinate? If not, what do they need?

5 Most seeds in soil will germinate. After a few days, the baby plants will push through the soil.

6 Once the plants come up, measure their heights each day with a ruler. Keep a record of their growth like the one shown above. In which soil did plants grow best? Grow poorest?

Soils and Plants
An Explanation

Seeds can germinate without soil. Seeds have all the food a plant needs to germinate and begin to grow.

Green plants make their own food. They need only light, water, the right minerals, and a gas in air called carbon dioxide.

> **FACT:** Plants can grow without soil. They can be grown in water (hydroponics) as long as the water contains the minerals the plants need.

The results of your experiments will differ. Results depend on the seeds you used, how long you measured the plants, and on the minerals in the soils you use. Sand and gravel often lack minerals that plants need to grow. As a result, plants grown in sand or gravel may not grow well. Plants grow best in soil that is a mixture of clay, silt, sand, and organic matter.

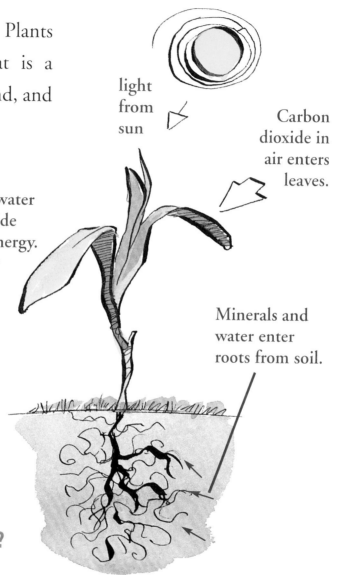

light from sun

Carbon dioxide in air enters leaves.

Plants combine water and carbon dioxide using the sun's energy. This is how they make food.

Minerals and water enter roots from soil.

Idea for Your Science Fair

- Do light and temperature, as well as water and soil, affect the growth of plants? Do experiments to find out.

9

Making Water Rise

How do you think you can make water rise? Write down your ideas and your reasons for them.

Now Let's Find Out!

1 Pour an inch of water into a tall clear glass and add several drops of food coloring. Use scissors to cut a strip from a paper towel. Make the strip about an inch wide. Cut across the width of the towel.

2 Hang the strip above the water using a pencil and tape as shown. The lower end of the strip should touch the water. Watch what happens. Did water rise up the paper towel?

3 Have **an adult** cut the bottom off a clear plastic cup. This will make a tube that is open at both ends.

4 Put the tube in an aluminum pie pan. Fill the tube with white sand.

5 Add about an inch of water to the pan. Watch closely. What happens? Does water rise up through the sand? Does it rise higher than the water in the pan? If it does, how can this help plants grow?

6 Leave the tube of sand in the soil over night. How high will the water rise?

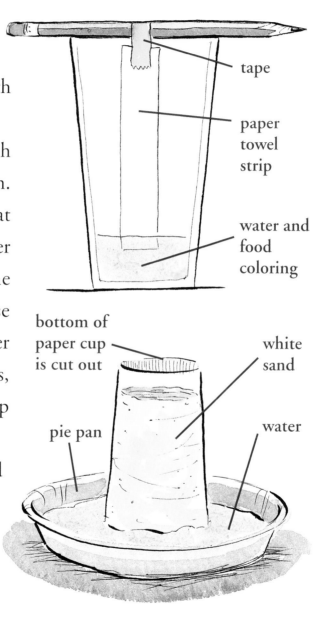

tape

paper towel strip

water and food coloring

bottom of paper cup is cut out

white sand

pie pan

water

Making Water Rise
An Explanation

There are narrow spaces between paper towel fibers and between particles of soil. Water creeps in and fills these narrow spaces. It rises up or moves sideways along these tiny openings. It does this because water is attracted to paper and soil. But particles of water are also attracted to each other. As a result, they hang together as water "climbs" up narrow spaces.

Will the water stop climbing? Yes! It stops when the weight of the water equals its attraction to the narrow surfaces

FACT: There are strong attractive forces between water particles. Water holds together so well that insects can walk on its surface. Paper clips can rest on its surface and not sink.

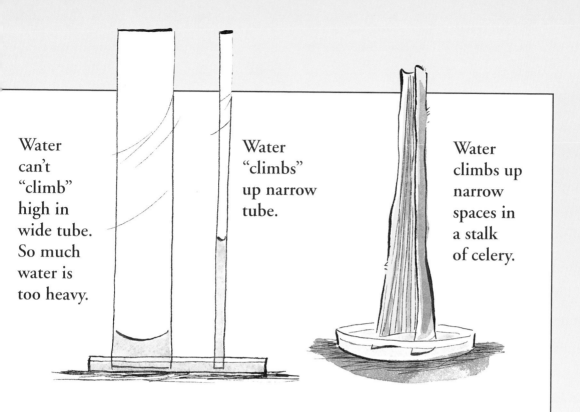

Water can't "climb" high in wide tube. So much water is too heavy.

Water "climbs" up narrow tube.

Water climbs up narrow spaces in a stalk of celery.

and to itself. This movement of water is called *capillary action.* Capillary action brings deeper water up to the roots of plants.

Idea for Your Science Fair

- Nearly fill a clear drinking glass with sand. Place a pie tin on the glass. Have an adult hold the pan against the glass and turn it upside down. You now have a tube of sand closed at the top. Add water to the pan. Watch closely several times each hour. Does water rise up the sand? How do the results here compare with those using the open tube of sand? Can you explain any differences?

10

Moving Soil with Water

Do you think water can wash away soil? Write down your ideas and your reasons for them.

Now Let's Find Out!

Do this experiment outdoors.

1 Nearly fill a clear, disposable, plastic paint tray with soil. Garden soil will do.

2 Get scissors and a sheet of white paper. Cut a circular hole about 4 inches (10 centimeters) wide in the center of the paper. Place the paper on the soil.

3 Use a brick or wood blocks to raise the deep end of the tray. Raise it 4 or 5 inches. Put several sheets of newspaper under the lower end of the tray.

THINGS YOU WILL NEED:
- clear, disposable, plastic paint tray
- soil, such as garden soil
- scissors
- white paper
- brick or wood blocks
- newspaper
- watering can
- grassy sod, if possible

4 Use a watering can to "rain" on the circular hole in the paper. Does the "rain" move any of the soil? How can you tell?

5 Remove the paper with the hole. Then "rain" all over the soil. What collects on the newspaper? Do you think rain can make soil move?

6 If possible, replace the soil with grassy sod. Put a clean newspaper under the low end of the tray. Then "rain" on the grassy soil. What is different this time? What is one way to reduce soil on hillsides from washing away? In what other ways might water move soil?

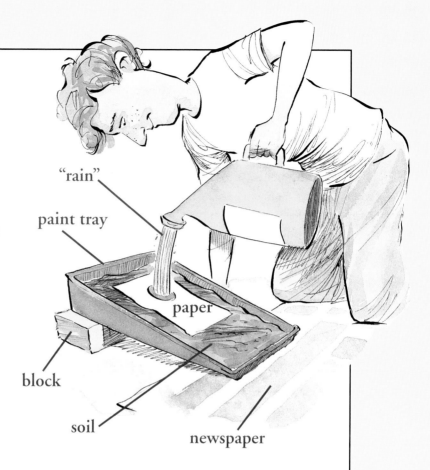

"rain"

paint tray

paper

block

soil

newspaper

Moving Soil with Water
An Explanation

You saw that rain can move (erode) soil. Soil moved onto the white paper when you "rained" on the soil. And soil moved down the slope and collected on the newspaper. The same thing happens in nature. Rain can cause soil to erode. Water can move soil down hillsides. The moving water in rivers, brooks, and oceans can also cause soil to erode.

You saw that grass or other plants can keep soil in place. The roots of plants help hold soil in place.

FACT: Making terraces on hillsides by leveling portions of a slope can reduce soil erosion.

Gullies are made
by rain running
down a hillside.

washed soil
from hillside

Idea for Your Science Fair

- Look for eroded soil in your neighborhood. Figure out ways to reduce the erosion.

Words to Know

aquifer—Underground rock or soil where the spaces between soil particles are filled with water. Wells are often drilled into aquifers to provide drinking water.

bedrock—The solid rock that lies under soil. Water cannot pass through it.

capillary action—The movement of liquids, like water, into and along narrow spaces. The liquids rise until the forces of attraction are balanced by the water's weight.

erosion—The movement of soil by water, wind, or gravity.

evaporation—The change of a liquid into a gas. The higher the temperature, the faster the liquid evaporates.

germination—The first growth of a baby plant from a seed.

organic matter—The remains of living things.

sediments—Rock particles carried by water, ice, or wind that settle out as layers.

soil—The mineral particles—clay, silt, sand, and gravel—and organic matter that cover parts of Earth's land surface.

weathering—The process in which water, wind, temperature changes, and other things slowly break rocks into small particles.

Further Reading

Books

Cobb, Vicki. *I Get Wet.* New York: HarperCollins, 2002.

Dispezio, Michael A. *Super Sensational Science Fair Projects.* New York: Sterling Publishing, 2002.

Ditchfield Christen. *Water.* New York: Children's Press, 2002.

Halfmann, Janet. *Life Under a Stone.* Mankato, Minn.: Creative Education, 2000.

Hammersmith, Craig. *Rising Up, Falling Down.* Minneapolis, Minn.: Compass Point Books, 2002.

Nankivell-Aston, Sally and Dorothy Jackson. *Science Experiments with Water.* New York: Franklin Watts, 2000.

Stewart, Melissa. *Soil.* Crystal Lake, Ill.: Heinemann Library, 2002.

Internet Addresses

Plant Experiments for Kids
<http://www.mgonline.com/experimentsforkids.html>

The Water Cycle
<http://www.kidzone.ws/water/>

Index